MW01148312

Printed in the United States of America

First Printing, 2020

Published by BookBaby
www.bookbaby.com

theworthyreminders@gmail.com

This book is dedicated to each and every one of you. May you always know your worth.

Love, CoCo

Hey, you!

Yes, you sitting right there.

Did you know that you are WORTHY?

WELL, YOU ARE!

What is worthy, you ask?

I'M SO EXCITED TO TELL YOU!

W

Worthy means that you're amazing just because you were born!

○

Oh, how UNIQUE AND SPECIAL YOU ARE!

R

Remember that you are deserving of love and respect at all times!

T

TRULY, YOU
ARE IMPORTANT AND
WORTHY OF GOOD THINGS!

H

HONORING YOURSELF, AND
ALLOWING OTHERS TO HONOR YOU,
IS WORTHWHILE.

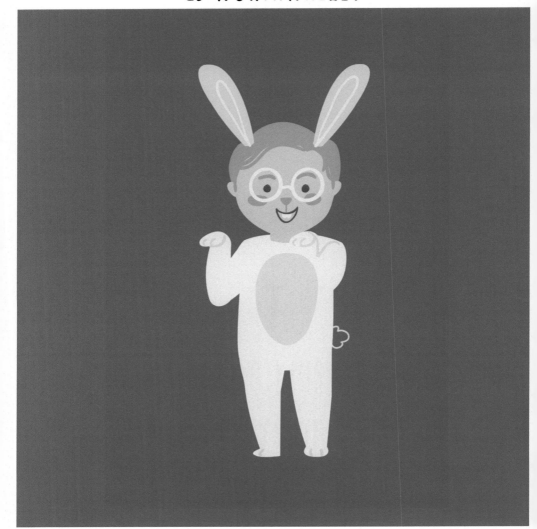

kind   special

smart

worthy

funny

Loved

unique

Y

YOU ARE
THE VERY BEST!
(I left space above for you to put your own words!)

Being worthy means that you are more than good enough!

Now tell yourself every day, "I am WORTHY!"

Do you know who else is worthy?

Moms are worthy!

Dads are worthy!

Sisters are
worthy!

Brothers are worthy!

So now you know! Everyone, including YOU, was born worthy and unique to share their talents with the world.